Music Arou...

By Teresa Domnauer

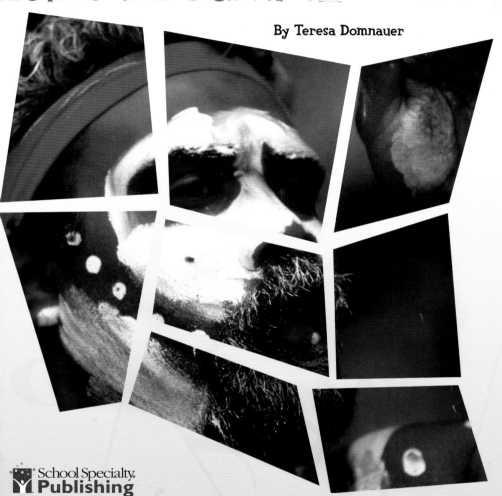

School Specialty Publishing

Library of Congress Cataloging-in-Publication Data is on file with the publisher.

Send all inquiries to:
School Specialty Publishing
8720 Orion Place
Columbus, OH 43240-2111

ISBN 0-7696-4223-3

1 2 3 4 5 6 7 8 9 10 PHXBK 10 09 08 07 06 05

Table of Contents

Australia

Aborigines were the first
people to live in Australia.
They moved there from
Southeast Asia.
They still live there today.
Singing is important to the aborigines.
They sing songs for love, good health,
and hunting.
The aborigines have songs
that only men sing.
They have songs that only women sing.
They have passed down these songs
from **generation** to generation.
They also play musical instruments.
One of these instruments is the didgeridoo.

Farkle Fact

A didgeridoo is made from a hollow log. It is played like a horn. Some didgeridoos can be up to 15 feet long!

Africa

Music is at the heart
of African people's lives.
It is a part of almost everything
they do.
There are songs to help babies fall asleep.
There are songs for children
and the games they play.
There are songs for working and for hunting.
African people play music for weddings
and for funerals.
African people believe that the drum
is a special, powerful instrument.
Musicians play many different drums
at the same time.

Farkle Fact

Many African songs feature something known as the "call-and-response." One person sings. Then, another person sings an answer to that person.

The Middle East

Music has been an important part of Middle Eastern **culture** for thousands of years.
Paintings from long ago in Egypt show musicians playing flutes and stringed instruments.
People in the Middle East still play these instruments today.
One of these instruments is the lute.
The body of the lute is shaped like a pear.
Its sounds are smooth and soft.

Farkle Fact

In the Middle East, special songs tell people when it is time to pray.

India

The raga is the most important
part of Indian music.
A raga is a short tune.
Each Indian raga means something special.
Some ragas tell about feelings,
such as happiness or sadness.
Others tell about a time of day,
such as morning or night.
Two important Indian instruments
are the tabla and the sitar.
The tabla is a small, round drum.
The sitar has a long neck and many strings.
Indian musicians sit on the floor
as they play these instruments.

Farkle Fact

Talas are Indian rhythms. The word *tala* means
"to clap hands."

Japan

Taiko drumming comes
from Japan.
The taiko drum has been played
there for thousands of years.
Its deep, loud sounds were first used
to scare enemies in battle.
Today, groups of drummers **perform**
this music.
The drummers have strong arms.
They pound quickly on the drums.
The sounds rumble like thunder.
A taiko show is very exciting.
Sometimes, the drummers yelp
while they play!

Farkle Fact
The word *taiko* means "fat drum."

Scotland

The bagpipe is the most
important instrument
in Scottish music.
It is a wind instrument.
Players blow air into the bags on a bagpipe
as they squeeze them.
The bagpipe player makes long, high notes
by covering different openings as the air
is squeezed out.
Bagpipe players from Scotland
wear plaid **kilt** skirts.
Many Scottish people dance
to the tunes of the bagpipes.

Farkle Fact

Another popular instrument in Scotland is the fiddle.
Playing the fiddle has been a **tradition** in Scotland
for a long time.

Italy

Many years ago, people began
to put on plays in Italy.
The actors in the plays sang the words
of the story instead of speaking them.
These plays are operas.
While walking through an Italian city,
you might hear the voices of opera singers.
Parts of Italy have warm weather
all year long.
This means that operas can be
performed outdoors.
Operas are also performed in **opera houses**.
A very famous opera house in Italy
is La Scala.

Farkle Fact

An opera in China is very different from an opera
in Italy. Some Chinese operas include puppets. They also
have acrobats that flip through the air.

Austria

Austria is called
"the land of music."
Many famous **composers**
were born there.
Many other composers moved there
to live and work.
Austria is home to choirs, **orchestras**,
and **theaters**.
It also has two famous opera houses.
In the summer, there are music **festivals**
throughout the country.
Students come from all over the world
to study at the music schools in Austria.

Farkle Fact

The famous composer Wolfgang Mozart was born
in Austria. He began writing music when he was only
five years old. When he was six, Mozart played for the
Queen of Austria!

The Caribbean Islands

The Caribbean Islands are
surrounded by clear ocean waters.
Calypso music comes from
this sunny area.
This kind of music is often played at parties.
Its happy rhythms and quick beats
make people want to dance.
Steel drums are an important part
of calypso music.
These large drums sound like
little xylophones.
Calypso bands also have singers, guitar
players, and flute players.

Farkle Fact

The first steel drums were made from garbage can lids
and cookie tins.

Mexico

Music and dance are
very important to the people
of Mexico.
One type of Mexican music is mariachi.
Musicians who play this music
are mariachis.
They sing and play guitars, trumpets,
and violins.
They stroll along the streets as they play.
Mariachis also play for people
in public places.
Sometimes, they play gentle love songs.
Other times, they play fast songs
with fast rhythms.

Farkle Fact

In Mexico, people dance the Mexican Hat Dance
at parties. This is a happy folk dance. People hop and
tap their feet as they dance around a hat.

Native America

For Native Americans,
music is a part of life.
They play music to help make
sick people feel better.
They play music for celebrations,
for hunting, and for rain.
Native Americans sing songs.
They play drums, rattles, and flutes.
Native Americans also dance.
Their dances copy the way
that animals in nature move.

Farkle Fact

A powwow is a special Native American celebration.
Music is a big part of a powwow. Many tribes come
together to sing, dance, and have fun.

New Orleans, Louisiana

Jazz music began in
New Orleans, Louisiana,
almost one hundred years ago.
It began as a combination of blues,
ragtime, and marching music.
Many jazz musicians still play
in New Orleans.
They play jazz on the sidewalk.
They play jazz in restaurants
and nightclubs.

Farkle Fact

Louis Armstrong was born in New Orleans. He was one
of the most famous jazz musicians who ever lived.

America

Music has always been
important to people in America.
But America is probably most famous
for being the birthplace of rock and roll.
Rock-and-roll music started in America
about 50 years ago.
It was a mixture of country music
and the blues.
But rock and roll was different.
It had a stronger beat.
It was fun for dancing.
Soon, young people all around the world
listened to rock and roll.
It is still popular today.

Farkle Fact

England is an important place for rock and roll, too.
It is the home of such famous rock stars as the Beatles
and the Rolling Stones.

Vocabulary

composer–a person who writes music. *Mozart was a famous composer from Austria.*

culture–the way of life for a group of people, including their ideas, arts, and traditions. *Music and dance are important to Native American culture.*

festival–an event that celebrates something special. *We go to the music festival every summer.*

generation–a group of people born and living at about the same time. *My grandfather's generation was alive when Louis Armstrong performed.*

kilt–a plaid wool skirt worn by men in Scotland. *The Scottish bagpipe players wore red and green kilts.*

musician–a person who plays music. *That musician plays the lute.*

perform–to put on a show. *The jazz band performs every night.*

opera house–a theater where opera is performed. *Many famous opera singers perform at the Sydney Opera House in Australia.*

orchestra–a group of musicians with sections of string, brass, woodwind, and percussion players. *The orchestra played the music for the ballet.*

theater–a large space with a stage for performers and seats for viewers. *We went to the theater to see the orchestra play.*

tradition–a belief or custom passed on from generation to generation. *It is a tradition to dance the Mexican Hat Dance at celebrations.*

Think About It!

1. In what country might you see a band of bagpipe players?

2. What does a mariachi band do?

3. In what city was jazz born?

4. Name two instruments that are from India.

5. What is the most important instrument in African music?

The Story and You!

1. Have you listened to music from another part of the world? Where did you hear it? Describe what the music sounded like.

2. This book talks about many different kinds of music. Which kind do you think you would like best? Why?

3. Are any of your friends or family members from another country? What kind of music do they listen to? Is it different from the music you listen to?

4. How is music a part of your life? When do you listen to music?

5. Do you know any songs in other languages? Talk about the songs and what the words mean.

Other *Lithgow Palooza*™ Readers your child can enjoy:

Level Two	Level Three	Level Four
weet, Oompa, Bumpety-Boom!	Music Around the World	Sing, Strum, and Beat the Drum!
Moo-Moo Went the Tuba	Sounds of Celebration!	Rock, Rag, and Swing

The FREE Educational Parent Newsletter:

Ve at School Specialty Publishing would like to help you make a difference
า the education of your child. We offer a **FREE** newsletter that provides
urrent topics on education and includes activities that you and your child
an work on together. Available in electronic format only.

o receive our **FREE** newsletter, please call us at **800-417-3261** or visit us
nline at **www.SchoolSpecialtyPublishing.com**.

lithgow
palooza readers

From aboriginal hunting songs in Australia to gentle mariachi love songs in Mexico, music is a part of people's everyday lives all around the world! John Lithgow is dedicated to introducing developing readers to the wonderful worlds of arts and literacy. Turn the page and join his character, Farkle McBride on a fascinating, fun reading adventure!

Guided Reading Level: M
Interest Level: 2–5

EMERGING READER   Grades K–1

EMERGING 2 READER

- repetitive language
- familiar and unfamiliar vocabulary
- longer sentences

CONFIDENT READER   Grades 1–2

CONFIDENT 3 READER

- minimal repetition
- challenging vocabulary; unfamiliar words
- varied, complex sentences

INDEPENDENT READER   Grades 2–3

INDEPENDENT 4 READER

- no repetition
- more complex vocabulary
- challenging sentence structure

U.S. $3.95
Can. $5.95

ISBN 0-7696-4223-3

ALIGNED TO STATE & NATIONAL STANDARDS!
SchoolSpecialtyPublishing.com

School Specialty Publishing

Visit our Web site at:
www.SchoolSpecialtyPublishing.com

0 87577 91923 2   04223

UPC

JENNY TAYLOR

Ronan
and
Juliette